EXCELLENCE IS NEVER
AN ACCIDENT

Stem-winders, jump-starters,
and joy bringers
to help you on the path
toward excellence

By Derric Johnson

Excellence Is Never An Accident
Stem-winders, jump-starters, and joy bringers
to help you on the path toward excellence
ISBN 1-57757-001-4

6th Printing - 2000

Copyright © 1997 by Derric Johnson
P. O. Box 944
Sherwood, Oregon 97140

Published by Trade Life Books, Inc.
P.O. Box 55325
Tulsa, OK 74155

Introduction

Excellence! For most of us, it's our challenge. It's our goal. It's our fervent desire. We want to be considered the best at what we do.

We want to be appreciated as a person of accomplishment — a person who excels, eclipses, surpasses, shines, and stands out in the crowd.

What makes the difference between a person of significance and a person of mediocrity? It's that slight edge of *Excellence!*

From page to page this delightful book is filled with inspiring and insightful quotes to assist and challenge you along on your personal path toward excellence.

Excellence Is Never An Accident is a book for today's aspiring achiever. It's *help* when you need it. it's that lift you've been looking for!

No matter what
accomplishments you make...
somebody helps you.

— *Althea Gibson*

If the grass is greener
on the other side of the fence...
it's time to fertilize your lawn!

♦ ♦ ♦

EXCELLENCE IS NEVER AN ACCIDENT

Man's mind once stretched
by a new idea...
never regains its original dimension.

— *Oliver Wendell Holmes*

EXCELLENCE IS NEVER AN ACCIDENT

You see things that are
and say, "Why?"
But I dream things that never were
and say, "Why not?"

— *George Bernard Shaw*

EXCELLENCE

B U I L D E R S

We attract what we expect;
We reflect what we desire;
We become what we respect;
We mirror what we admire.

◆ ◆ ◆

Imagination is more important
than knowledge.

— *Albert Einstein*

EXCELLENCE IS NEVER AN ACCIDENT

Curiosity keeps us moving forward,
exploring,
experimenting,
opening new doors.

— *Walt Disney*

◆ ◆ ◆

◆

Limits exist only in the souls
of those who do not dream.

◆ ◆ ◆

Conscience is what hurts...
when everything else feels good.

To see things in a seed...
that is vision.

◆ ◆ ◆

EXCELLENCE IS NEVER AN ACCIDENT

Why not go out on a limb?
Isn't that where the fruit is?

◆ ◆ ◆

EXCELLENCE IS NEVER AN ACCIDENT

High expectations
are the key to everything.

— *Sam Walton*

◆ ◆ ◆

B U I L D E R S

Experience is not
the best teacher...
it is the only teacher.

◆ ◆ ◆

If you want to feel rich...
just count all of the things you have...
that money can't buy.

◆ ◆ ◆

EXCELLENCE IS NEVER AN ACCIDENT

Always remember
that the best things in life
aren't things.

◆ ◆ ◆

If you play it safe in life,
you've decided you don't want
to grow anymore.

◆ ◆ ◆

The man on top
of the mountain
didn't fall there.

EXCELLENCE IS NEVER AN ACCIDENT

Creativity is finding new things...
or expressing old truths
in new ways.

— *Roger vol Oech*

♦ ♦ ♦

What the caterpillar calls "the end"...
the butterfly calls "the beginning."

♦ ♦ ♦

EXCELLENCE IS NEVER AN ACCIDENT

One of the greatest enemies
that we can ever face in life...
is the illusion that
there will be more time tomorrow
than there is today.

♦ ♦ ♦

EXCELLENCE

B U I L D E R S

When an archer misses the mark,
he turns and looks
for the fault within himself.
Failure to hit the bulls-eye
is never the fault of the target.

To improve your aim...
improve yourself.

◆ ◆ ◆

Reach for the possible...
not just the expected.

◆ ◆ ◆

EXCELLENCE IS NEVER AN ACCIDENT

You are young at any age...
if you're planning for tomorrow.

EXCELLENCE IS NEVER AN ACCIDENT

It is true that the present
is colored by the past...
it is also true we can choose
the colors of the future.

◆ ◆ ◆

Faith is not
trying to believe something
regardless of evidence.
Faith is daring to do something
regardless of the consequence.

◆ ◆ ◆

EXCELLENCE IS NEVER AN ACCIDENT

To understand the mind of a person,
look at what he has already achieved.
To understand the heart of a person,
look at what he aspires yet to do.

◆ ◆ ◆

EXCELLENCE IS NEVER AN ACCIDENT

Vision is the art
of seeing things invisible.

— *Jonathan Swift*

If you can dream it,
you can do it.

— *Walt Disney*

◆ ◆ ◆

EXCELLENCE IS NEVER AN ACCIDENT

I don't know
what your destiny will be...
but one thing I know...
the only ones among you
who will be really happy...
are those who will have
sought and found how to serve.

— *Dr. Albert Schweitzer*

◆ ◆ ◆

EXCELLENCE IS NEVER AN ACCIDENT

About the best use
I can find for life...
is to spend it on something
that will outlast me.

◆ ◆ ◆

B U I L D E R S

A smile is a silent laugh.
A grin is a smile to yourself that shows.
A chuckle is a small laugh,
sometimes real, sometimes not.
A snicker is a wicked chuckle.
A chortle is an old-time,
deep-down laugh.
And a laugh is the music of happiness.

◆ ◆ ◆

Regret of the past
and fear of the future...
are twin enemies of the soul.

◆ ◆ ◆

EXCELLENCE IS NEVER AN ACCIDENT

Without inspiration...
we would perish.

— *Walt Disney*

◆ ◆ ◆

EXCELLENCE IS NEVER AN ACCIDENT

The one who says
it cannot be done...
should never interrupt
the one who is doing it.

♦ ♦ ♦

EXCELLENCE IS NEVER AN ACCIDENT

If there be any truer measure of a man
than what he does...
it must be what he gives.

♦ ♦ ♦

There is no pillow as soft
as a clear conscience.

— *John Wooden*

To forgive
calls upon your love...
To forget
calls upon your strength.

I will permit no man
to narrow and degrade my soul
by making me hate him.

— *Booker T. Washington*

EXCELLENCE IS NEVER AN ACCIDENT

Ask less often,
"What's in it for me?"
and ask more often,
"What's in me for it?"

— *Dr. John Ed Mathison*

Success can be
another form of failure...
if we forget what our priorities are.

◆ ◆ ◆

EXCELLENCE

BUILDERS

Fame is a vapor,
Popularity an accident,
Riches take wings.
Only one thing endures...
CHARACTER.

◆ ◆ ◆

He who makes a mistake
and fails to correct it...
makes another.

◆ ◆ ◆

EXCELLENCE IS NEVER AN ACCIDENT

We are paid best
for the things
we do for nothing.

◆ ◆ ◆

He who criticizes
is seldom forgiven.
He who encourages
is seldom forgotten.

◆ ◆ ◆

EXCELLENCE IS NEVER AN ACCIDENT

Duty is a very personal thing...
It is what comes from knowing
the need to take action...
and not just a need
to urge others to do something.

— *Mother Teresa*

◆ ◆ ◆

EXCELLENCE IS NEVER AN ACCIDENT

The difference between
an error and a mistake...
depends on how long it takes you
to correct the error.

◆ ◆ ◆

EXCELLENCE IS NEVER AN ACCIDENT

If you try to improve another person
by setting a good example...
then you are really
improving two people.

◆ ◆ ◆

We judge ourselves
by what we feel capable of doing...
while others judge us
by what we have already done.

◆ ◆ ◆

There is no substitute
for intelligence...
The only thing
that comes close to it
is silence.

Everybody is good for something....
Even the worst of us
can serve as a bad example.

◆ ◆ ◆

EXCELLENCE

B U I L D E R S

Excellence can be attained if you...

risk more than others think is safe,

care more than others think is wise,

dream more than others think is practical,

expect more than others think is possible.

◆ ◆ ◆

You can't control
the length of your life...
but you can control
the width and depth.

◆ ◆ ◆

EXCELLENCE IS NEVER AN ACCIDENT

Pride makes us do things well...
but it is love that makes us
do them to perfection.

◆ ◆ ◆

Improvement begins with "I".

♦ ♦ ♦

People who are
resting on their laurels
are wearing them
on the wrong end.

◆ ◆ ◆

Smart people believe
only half of what they hear...
smarter people know
which half to believe.

◆ ◆ ◆

EXCELLENCE IS NEVER AN ACCIDENT

If you don't have time
to do it right...
when will you have time
to do it over?

◆ ◆ ◆

EXCELLENCE IS NEVER AN ACCIDENT

Wealth, like happiness,
is never attained
when sought after directly...
It always comes as a by-product
of providing a useful service.

— *Henry Ford*

◆ ◆ ◆

EXCELLENCE IS NEVER AN ACCIDENT

Rare is the person
who can weigh the faults of others
without putting his thumb
on the scales.

♦ ♦ ♦

Politeness is to human nature
what warmth is to wax.

◆ ◆ ◆

EXCELLENCE

B U I L D E R S

THINGS WORTH REMEMBERING...
The value of time.
The success of perseverance.
The dignity of simplicity.
The worth of character.
The virtue of patience.
The wisdom of economy.
The power of kindness.

◆ ◆ ◆

Real generosity
is doing something nice...
for someone
who'll never find it out.

◆ ◆ ◆

EXCELLENCE IS NEVER AN ACCIDENT

People often ask me
if I know the secret of success
and if I could tell others
how to make their dreams come true.
My answer is...
you do it by working.

— *Walt Disney*

♦ ♦ ♦

Forgiveness is
the fragrance the violet sheds
on the heel
that has crushed it.

◆ ◆ ◆

This is the final test
of a gentleman...
his respect for those
who can be of no
possible value to him.

◆ ◆ ◆

There's no right way
to do the wrong thing.

◆ ◆ ◆

It's not hard to make decisions
when you know what your values are.

— Roy Disney

Most people are about as happy
as they make up their minds to be.

— *Abraham Lincoln*

◆ ◆ ◆

EXCELLENCE IS NEVER AN ACCIDENT

The quality of a person's life
is in direct proportion
to his commitment to excellence...
regardless of the chosen
field of endeavor.

— *Vince Lombardi*

Success is
getting what you want....
Happiness is
liking what you get.

◆ ◆ ◆

EXCELLENCE

B U I L D E R S

Success is to be measured
not so much by the position
that one has reached in life...
as by the obstacles
that he has overcome
while trying to succeed.

◆ ◆ ◆

— Booker T. Washington

EXCELLENCE IS NEVER AN ACCIDENT

Most of us look at success
in the same positive way.
It's how we deal with our failures...
that determines
what we get out of life.

◆ ◆ ◆

EXCELLENCE IS NEVER AN ACCIDENT

Success comes in cans...
failure in can'ts.

◆ ◆ ◆

Nothing is all wrong.
Even a clock
that has stopped running...
is right twice a day.
Patience is the ability
to let your light shine
after your fuse has blown.

◆ ◆ ◆

EXCELLENCE IS NEVER AN ACCIDENT

If you stand up and are counted...
you may get knocked down.
But remember this....
A man flattened by an opponent
can get up again.
A man flattened by conformity
stays down for good.

◆ ◆ ◆

We are not here to pursue happiness...
but to pursue those virtues
that produce happiness.

◆ ◆ ◆

Enjoy the little things...
some day you will
look back and realize
they were the big things.

◆ ◆ ◆

The gift of happiness
belongs to those
who unwrap it.

◆ ◆ ◆

EXCELLENCE IS NEVER AN ACCIDENT

If you think that
the competitive spirit is dead...
just watch the customers
in a supermarket
when a cashier opens
a new checkout lane.

◆ ◆ ◆

When you hear people say
that life is hard,
always ask them,
"Compared to what?"

◆ ◆ ◆

EXCELLENCE

BUILDERS

Wisdom is knowing
what to do next...
skill is knowing
how to do it...
and virtue is doing it.

♦ ♦ ♦

EXCELLENCE IS NEVER AN ACCIDENT

Success is where preparation
and opportunity meet.

— *Bobby Unser*

◆ ◆ ◆

People who cross their bridges
before they come to them...
have to pay the toll twice.

If at first you succeed...
try to hide your astonishment.

◆ ◆ ◆

EXCELLENCE IS NEVER AN ACCIDENT

Winning is a habit.
Unfortunately, so is losing.

— Vince Lombardi

Coming together is beginning.
Keeping together is progress.
Working together is success.

— Henry Ford

◆ ◆ ◆

EXCELLENCE IS NEVER AN ACCIDENT

You make a living
from what you get...
but you make a life
from what you give.

EXCELLENCE IS NEVER AN ACCIDENT

The bigger we get...
the smaller we have to think.
Customers still walk in
one at a time.

— *Sam Walton*

Stress is what happens
when your gut says, "No"...
but your mouth says,
"Of course. I'd be glad to."

♦ ♦ ♦

Life is too short
to do everything necessary
to live longer.

◆ ◆ ◆

EXCELLENCE

B U I L D E R S

The way to gain
a good reputation...
is to endeavor to be
what you desire to appear.

♦ ♦ ♦

It doesn't matter
if you win or lose...
until you lose.

◆ ◆ ◆

EXCELLENCE IS NEVER AN ACCIDENT

Too many people grow up.
That's the real trouble
with the world....
They forget.
They don't remember
what it's like to be 12 years old.

— *Walt Disney*

◆ ◆ ◆

EXCELLENCE IS NEVER AN ACCIDENT

We cannot change the wind...
but we can adjust the sail.

◆ ◆ ◆

EXCELLENCE IS NEVER AN ACCIDENT

It's a funny thing about life...
if you refuse to accept
anything but the best
you very often get it.

◆ ◆ ◆

EXCELLENCE IS NEVER AN ACCIDENT

If it weren't for the rocks in its bed...
the stream would have no song.

◆ ◆ ◆

EXCELLENCE IS NEVER AN ACCIDENT

Why worry?
If you've done the very best you can...
worrying won't make it any better.

— *Walt Disney*

◆ ◆ ◆

Love isn't what makes
the world go around....
Love is what makes
the ride worthwhile.

◆ ◆ ◆

Never, never, never, never
give up.

— Winston Churchill

An optimist is someone who takes
the cold water thrown on his idea...
heats it with enthusiasm...
and uses the steam to push ahead.

EXCELLENCE

B U I L D E R S

Unless there is within us
that which is above us,
we shall soon yield to
that which is about us.

◆ ◆ ◆

Success seems to be largely
a matter of hanging on...
after others have let go.

◆ ◆ ◆

EXCELLENCE IS NEVER AN ACCIDENT

In the confrontation between
the stream and the rock,
the stream always wins...
not through strength
but by perseverance.

EXCELLENCE IS NEVER AN ACCIDENT

Resolve to perform
what you ought...
perform without fail
what you resolve.

— *Benjamin Franklin*

◆ ◆ ◆

Do not let what you cannot do...
interfere with what you can do.

— *John Wooden*

Don't be afraid to take a big step
if one is indicated...
you can't cross a chasm
in two small jumps.

◆ ◆ ◆

EXCELLENCE IS NEVER AN ACCIDENT

It is only when you are pursued
that you become swift.

— *Kahil Gibran*

Great spirits have
always encountered
violent opposition
from mediocre minds.

— *Albert Einstein*

◆ ◆ ◆

Whenever one acquires knowledge
but does not practice it...
it is like one who plows a field...
but does not sow it.

◆ ◆ ◆

Every time you graduate
from the school of experience...
someone thinks up a new course.

◆ ◆ ◆

Only brag about what
you're going to do tomorrow...
when you did what
you were going to do yesterday.

◆ ◆ ◆

EXCELLENCE IS NEVER AN ACCIDENT

It is not possible for a person to be
what he ought to be...
until he does
what he ought to be doing.

◆ ◆ ◆

The quickest way
to become an old dog...
is to stop learning new tricks.

♦ ♦ ♦

The measure of success
is not whether you have
a tough problem to deal with...
but whether it's the same problem
you had last year.

◆ ◆ ◆

EXCELLENCE IS NEVER AN ACCIDENT

Winning is not a sometime thing...
it's an all-time thing.
You don't win once in a while,
you don't do things right
once in a while...
you do them right all the time.

— *Vince Lombardi*

◆ ◆ ◆

Life can only be understood
backwards...
but it must be lived
forwards.

◆ ◆ ◆

Those who make
the worst use of their time...
are the first to complain
of its shortness.

◆ ◆ ◆

God loves you just the way you are...
but He loves you too much
to let you stay that way.

◆ ◆ ◆

EXCELLENCE IS NEVER AN ACCIDENT

There is a difference between
perseverance and obstinacy...
one is a strong will
and the other is a strong won't.

♦ ♦ ♦

The right to be heard is
constitutionally guaranteed.
The right to be listened to
must be earned.

◆ ◆ ◆

EXCELLENCE

B U I L D E R S

The special secret of making dreams
come true is summarized in four C's.

Curiosity
Confidence
Courage
Constancy

and the greatest of these is Confidence.

— *Walt Disney*

One thing about experience
is that when you don't
have very much...
you're apt to get a lot.

◆ ◆ ◆

EXCELLENCE IS NEVER AN ACCIDENT

I couldn't wait for success...
so I went ahead without it.

— *Jonathan Winters*

◆ ◆ ◆

I worry about many things...
but not about water over the dam.

— *Walt Disney*

◆ ◆ ◆

Never confuse motion with action...
and never confuse action
with accomplishment.

◆ ◆ ◆

EXCELLENCE IS NEVER AN ACCIDENT

The only successful substitute
for work is a miracle.

◆ ◆ ◆

Don't be afraid
to ask dumb questions...
they're easier to handle
than dumb mistakes.

◆ ◆ ◆

It is more important to know
where you're going...
than to get there fast.

◆ ◆ ◆

Life is like riding a bicycle...
you don't fall off
unless you stop pedaling.

◆ ◆ ◆

What's the difference
between school and life?
In school, you're taught a lesson
and then given a test.
In life, you're given a test
that teaches you a lesson.

◆ ◆ ◆

EXCELLENCE

BUILDERS

We shall be remembered more for...
our kindness than for
our accomplishments,
our generosity than for our riches,
our service than for our successes.

◆ ◆ ◆

EXCELLENCE IS NEVER AN ACCIDENT

I have been up against
tough competition all my life...
I wouldn't know
how to get along without it.

— *Walt Disney*

EXCELLENCE IS NEVER AN ACCIDENT

If a man advances confidently
in the direction of his dreams...
to live the life he has imagined...
he will meet with a success
unexpected in common hours.

— *Henry David Thoreau*

◆ ◆ ◆

Today's mighty oak is merely
yesterday's little nut...
that managed to hold its ground.

The well of creativity
never runs dry...
as long as you go to it.

— Dr. Orval C. Butcher

Keep living, dreaming,
loving, and risking.
More people rust out
than wear out.

Well done is better
than well said.

— *Ben Franklin*

Difficulties mastered
are opportunities won.

— *Winston Churchill*

◆ ◆ ◆

We can easily forgive a child
who is afraid of the dark...
the real tragedy of life is when
men are afraid of the light.

◆ ◆ ◆

We don't know
who we are
until we see
what we can do.

♦ ♦ ♦

EXCELLENCE

BUILDERS

Service is love made visible.
Friendship is love made personal.
Music is love made audible.
Kindness is love made tangible.
Giving is love made believable.

◆ ◆ ◆

Years wrinkle the skin...
but to give up enthusiasm
wrinkles the soul.

◆ ◆ ◆

There's a big difference
between nearly right
and exactly right.

◆ ◆ ◆

EXCELLENCE IS NEVER AN ACCIDENT

The nice thing about being young
is that you have not
experienced enough to know
you cannot possibly do
all the things you are doing.

◆ ◆ ◆

EXCELLENCE IS NEVER AN ACCIDENT

It is not easy to be crafty
and winsome at the same time...
and few there be who accomplish it
after the age of six!

Opportunity's
favorite disguise
is trouble.

◆ ◆ ◆

It is not until
pain exceeds fear
that we risk change.

The world expects results.
Don't tell others
about the labor pains...
show them the baby.

♦ ♦ ♦

EXCELLENCE

B U I L D E R S

EFFICIENCY
is doing things right.

EFFECTIVENESS
is doing right things.

EXCELLENCE
is doing right things right.

◆ ◆ ◆

The road to success is not
doing 1 thing 100% better...
but doing 100 things 1% better.

◆ ◆ ◆

Be early if you're a bird...
and late if you're a worm!

♦ ♦ ♦

Workers of the world arise...
you have nothing to lose
but your chairs.

◆ ◆ ◆

EXCELLENCE IS NEVER AN ACCIDENT

If you want your dreams
to come true...
the first thing you have to do
is wake up!

◆ ◆ ◆

About the Author

Derric Johnson epitomizes creativity. Renowned for excellence in talent and achieve-ment as a motivational speaker, ordained pastor, prolific songwriter, musician, creative consultant, and author. Derric brings life and artistic genius to everything he does. He is a Stanley Foundation Lecturer, featured nationally and inter-nationally. Over the past 20 years, he has served 18 years as a minister, authored 4 books, written 150 original songs, 23 cantatas, and 2800 musical arrangements, published 32 books of choral collections, with involvement in the production of 94 recorded albums on 12 labels. He founded and directed The Regeneration, a touring ensemble of singers who traveled 12 years, over one million miles,

performing to more than 12 million people in 6,000 concerts. Derric has been a specialty writer for Radio City Music Hall, and for the past 20 years, he has served as a Creative Consultant for Walt Disney World, currently arranging, producing, and staffing EPCOT Center's *The Voices of Liberty*.

For additional information on seminars, consulting services, scheduling speaking engagements, or to write the author, please address your correspondence to:

Derric Johnson
P. O. Box 944
Sherwood, Oregon 97140
Or call: 1-503-625-1539

Additional copies of this book and other portable titles
from Trade Life Books are available at your local bookstore.

Trade Life Books, Inc.
Tulsa, Oklahoma